Where Is My Mentor?

Angelene Crecy-Hill

Publisher: PIAOTT Publishing & Graphic Design LLC. Chicago, IL
Where Is My Mentor?
Angelene Crecy-Hill
© 2020   Printed in the United States of America
ISBN: 978-1-7362522-1-5

No part of this book may be recorded or transmitted in any form or by any means, electronic mechanical, including photocopying, recording, or by an information storage and retrieval system, without permission in writing from the publisher.

Table of Contents

Dedication 7

Foreword 9

Prologue 11

<u>CHAPTER</u>

   1 Midwife, Mentor or Coach 17

   2 Finding Angelene 25

   3 The Experience 31

   4 The Mentor In You 41

   5 Who Do You Mentor? 49

   6 Finding A Mentor 57

   7 The Mentor and Mentee 63

Afterword 67

For Further Reading 71

I dedicate this work to my husband Perry;

You have supported and stood by me through the thick and the thin. You endured the day, weeks, months, and years of frustration as I sought to figure out what the Lord was doing in me and what he wanted from me.
To my family, thank you for believing in me as you watch me throw in the towel, and God threw it back to me.
Love you forever!

Foreword

It is with much pleasure that I am writing the foreword for this author, who is my wife and partner in ministry. In this book, you will find a design that will connect the reader to a mentor's characteristics. You will also discover why it is a moral compulsion to seek the guidance of a mentor. As a mentor myself with thirty years of mentorship experience, I am assured and capable of writing the author's foreword. I thank her for choosing me.

As you are inspired to write, embark upon a new career, go back to school, relocate, seek advice in a relationship, or perhaps acknowledge the Call into ministry, etc., there will be times you will need guidance for moving forward as well as how and when to move at the proper time. The author offers a pathway for seeking the right mentor while expressing the importance of mentoring is for the betterment of your endeavor. This book will show how to find a mentor that will influence you in the right direction. You will also find the spiritual and natural giftings of God's power.

Where Is My Mentor? Encourages, admonishes, warns, and provide spiritual support to the reader. The author establishes the mentor and mentee's responsibilities through scripture and solidifies the roles of each with examples of the mentor/mentee relationship. She also proposes to the reader to connect to the mentor within themselves. This book will guide you toward finding the mentor that will help you accomplish your desired success. The appropriate mentor is capable of thrusting a mentee into the outcome he or she desires leading to life changing experiences.

Pastor Perry Hill
SFC Army, Retired

PROLOGUE

I pen this message to my brothers and sisters everywhere to inspire and confirm that everyone needs a mentor. As we journey in our Christian walk and through life, we encounter many things. We experience things that are perhaps common knowledge, while others may be more complicated. It is fortunate, with an amount of pondering, we may figure it out. On the contrary, there are times we come to a fork in the road that requires us to decide which way do I go? At this moment, it is crucial to have someone in your life who can speak words of life, give directions, and pray as you move confidently toward God's call. Every successful person has been or is connected to persons of success in some manner. This is not to suggest what success looks like, but it is to say that we need someone in our lives to help us get to where we are going in life.

My experience has inspired me to pen this message to you; there is someone in your proximity called to walk with you on your journey. You have first to acknowledge you need someone to help you in the areas that are not clear; then, understand the importance of a mentor and submit to the guidance provided.

We are in critical times; emotions are clouding out visions while uncertainties are over-ruling the confidence that was once prevalent in life's journey. These are the times when we glean from the sources provided in the Body of Christ to empower us to finish strong. Our instinct as believers is to run to the Word of God. It is our hiding place. The Word's manifestation is not only written on the pages of God's eternal Word; it is also the deeds and the obedience of believers who carry out the command of God to do, to be, and to say what he instructs. In that obedience is the lifeline to someone's cry for help. The help needed often is in the shape of guidance. It is at this time we embrace the scripture that "two are better than one" (Ecclesiastes 4:9); you are not alone; God has the mentor he has assigned to you.

If you are not cognizant of who has been assigned to guide you, ask God to allow your paths to cross. Chances are the person is already in your circle of influence, your paths have already crossed, or you will meet them in the near future. It is God's Will that we prosper and be in health even as our souls prosper (3 John 1:2).

The position of a mentor is, as the bible states, first natural, then spiritual. But based on the need of the Holy Spirit for guidance, a spiritual connection can sometimes supersede natural selection. A mentor does not or should not instruct based on what he or she feels. The instructions that will lead to a positive outcome has to be instructions from the Lord. Scripture ensures us that acknowledging the Higher Authority yields the fruit of righteousness. "Trust in the Lord with all thine heart; and lean not unto thine own understanding. In all thy ways acknowledge him, and he shall direct thy paths. Be not wise in thine own eyes; fear the Lord" (Proverbs 3:5-7).

New ministries are increasingly on the rise. We must answer the Call of God in this hour. Lives are hanging in the balance, and hell is enlarging herself. It is in this place, Jesus proclaimed, "And other sheep I have, which are not of this fold: them also I must bring, and they shall hear my voice: and there shall be one fold, and one shepherd"

(John 10:16). Mentees, call for your mentor. Mentor, answer the call to provide spiritual guidance. Be willing to spend time in prayer with and for a mentee. Be ready to stand in the gap as an intercessor for the new ministry leader; help the mentee get footage and gain leverage on the grounds of a new ministry, give precise instructions to a mentee who is making a significant decision in life. Mentors avail as a vessel of God. Be that vessel for the Masters' use. The pressure for wisdom is like we have not seen it before. Where Is My Mentor?

CHAPTER 1

Midwife, Mentor or Coach

The role of a Mentor, a Life Coach, or a Midwife are positions of influence designed to assists people in their endeavor to move forward. The encounters and life experiences often do not offer a clear-cut path to travel; therefore, it becomes necessary to seek guidance needed to move from one place to another. A Counselor, a Midwife, and a Mentor all have skills essential to the helping field. The three can be interchangeable, giving credit to the significance; each has a specific focal point in one's life.

> *Midwife - a person who assists women through pregnancy and childbirth and brings forth life, production, and increase. The midwife's role is typically carried out in the first stages of life. A midwife is known for assisting in childbearing; however, a spiritual midwife is instrumental in "bringing forth" in other life areas. Like the birthing midwife, a spiritual midwife can see what the birth-giver cannot. This life could be human life, the life of a new business, new career, or ministry. In any case, a good foundation is needed for a healthy outcome. A spiritual midwife facilitates the birth of new spiritual directions, unique gifts, or spiritual calling that a person may not know they possess.*

Coach - councils, guides, leads, mentors, and tutors. The role of a coach lends to short term assistance. A coach provides step-by-step instruction and support to motivate clients to move from where they are to where they desire to be. According to the definition of a coach, he or she assists a person in various professional areas based on performance. A coach's job is to improve one's performance on a professional level. There are numerous coaching cultures, including life coach, business coach, leadership coach, nutrition coach, marriage and family coach, health and wellness coach, financial coach, career coach, education coach, and the list. There are three coaching styles autocratic, democratic, and holistic. The individual has to choose what is appropriate for them or seek out information that will steer them in the right direction for selecting a coach. Coaching relationships are frequently limited to brief periods based on the need or expectation.

Mentor - a trusted counselor or guide, tutor, dedicated to assisting in guidance and providing everyday life instructions and wisdom. A mentor and mentee relationship can span for a lifetime based on the mentee's goal and expectations. A mentor's role serves on a more intimate level; as defined above, a mentor is a trusted counselor, a guide, and a tutor to assist one in a specific area of his or her life. After building a trusting relationship, the mentor's goal is to provide the mentee the guidance requested. A mentor can be both a spiritual and a natural advisor.

MENTORSHIP AND WHY IT'S NEEDED!

Defined as "a wise and trusted counselor or teacher," the Bible does not use the term mentorship. To the benefit of the readers, it gives several instances where men and women were mentors. One of the first instances of mentoring in the old testament is the example of Jethro and Moses. There are several things that we can learn about mentoring from their relationship in Exodus 18.

First, a solid foundation of mentorship is derived from a position of trust, (Exodus 18:1-8). In these verses, we see the bond of the mentor and mentee. They greeted one another, were concerned about one another's affairs, and spent time continually sharing their experiences. No doubt, this relationship had been cultivated with patience and love. Jethro knew that Moses was a shepherd in the wilderness, (Exodus 3:1).

Secondly, a mentoring relationship warrants transparency and honesty, (Exodus 18:8). Often, a significant amount of attention is given to the mentoring process than to the mentoring relationship. Without a relationship built by trust, love, and mutual commitment, the relationship can be sabotaged. Moses was willing to share his experiences (Moses told his father-in-law all that the Lord had done.) He also allowed himself to be vulnerable. Moses openly admitted his fears, mistakes, and concerns; Jethro was just as transparent.

Thirdly, the mentor genuinely desires the best for his protégé, (Exodus 18: Matthew 12). He or she knows the outcome is not based on the mentor's skills and gifts. On the contrary, all abilities and giftings are from God; we give him the accolades. Celebrate the successes of those you mentor while giving God glory. The mentor should be the biggest cheerleader of the mentee. It provides excellent satisfaction to the mentor to see the parade of success of the mentees. Mentors should only brag on how God uses them "for his glory." Jethro was very excited about how God blessed Moses. He saw Moses's victory as his own and was genuinely happy when things went well for him. Jethro was just as excited, if not more excited than Moses. Because of what God had done for him, Jethro threw a big feast for Moses, Aaron, and all the elders of Israel to show his rejoicing of God's plan. Jethro mentored Moses, Joshua, and the elders of Israel, and Eli mentored Samuel.

The book of Esther, chapter 2, gives the story of Esther and her Uncle Mordecai. Mordecai mentored Esther for her presentation to King Ahasuerus. He instructed her how to work out the God-ordained purpose of her life with the King. Her humility and submission to Mordecai's instructions brought forth the outcome she desired. Esther had not yet revealed anything to her kindred nor her people, as Mordecai had charged her: Esther did the commandment of Mordecai, like as when she was brought up with him (Esther 2:20).

In Titus's book, chapter 2 is given an account of spiritual mothering (a form of mentoring). The more mature women are admonished to guide the younger women in their everyday living as becoming women of God without reproach, without lying, to be mothers to their children, to be wives to their husbands, and to live their lives unspotted and without ridicule. Titus, chapter two also admonishes the older men to walk out a godly lifestyle that the younger men will know what godliness looks like. The younger men are to live sober-minded, having sound speech that cannot be condemned, and no one will have anything evil to say about them. The younger men will undoubtedly know what God desires of them, just as the older women are examples to the younger women and how honorable women should desire to live.

These godly characteristics are for both the younger men and younger women. In this passage, we are to show the generation that will come after us how to live a godly lifestyle. Myles Munroe quoted, "the greatest act of leadership is mentoring; no matter how much you may learn, achieve, accumulate, or accomplish, if it all dies with you, then you are a generational failure." In a mentor-mentee relationship, the leader is willing to pour into the mentee's life; the passing of the baton is the sole purpose and goal of a mentor (betterment). The mentor breathes life into the mentee; this breath will be the same breath that will be imparted into another generation's life. It does not stop at one; one is empowered that he or she may empower another one. A good mentor does not have to seek mentees; mentees are attracted to the nature of a good mentor; there is a fragrance on the Call of mentorship that is detected only by seeking guidance, directions, and instructions.

CHAPTER 2

Finding Angelene

My name is Mary Angelene Crecy-Hill. I am a native of Fayetteville, NC., the fourth of seven children born to Ms. Blanche L. Crecy; I am a mother of three, the grandmother of ten, and the wife of retired Army Sergeant First Class Perry Hill. At age 21, I gave my life to the Lord.

Unrecognizable, unexpectedly, and unwillingly, I was called into ministry. Being incognizant of what God was doing in my life, I did not recognize it was the "Call" until the age of 29. I did not know that obedience to God was not an option, especially to the Call to ministry. I thought you could say yes or no, and that would be the end of it. The consequences of my actions caused a chaotic mind that led to chaos in every area of my life. I entered a bubble of hitting and missing spiritually, and nothing seemed to work in my favor; this was happening from a place of blatant disobedience to what God wanted from my life. Little did I know, the Call for ministry and becoming a Military Wife was God's setup to prepare me for global ministry. I became aware and willing to submit to God's Call; it was in this position of humility that things began to fall in place.

My military wife life experience provided various opportunities to a worldview expansion. I recognized signs of religion versus relationship, "a different book." Therefore, I began to check things that did not line up with soul winning. The chains of a religious mentality were broken as I began to view life and people from multiple perspectives, mainly, a standpoint of "go ye therefore and teach all nations" (Matthew 28:19). It is indeed an honor that God can trust us with His spirit and do what he has assigned us to do; it is undoubtedly a privilege and an opportunity to do ministry with a global perspective. Understanding cultures, ethnic groups, geographical locations, and accepting differentiations is key to soul winning. The experience prepared me profoundly to provide a God-service to people of variations. Then said he unto his disciples, the harvest is plenteous, but the laborers are few, (Matthew 9:37).

While learning and appreciating "differences," as in ethnic groups, nationalities, culture variations, races, etc., I developed a desire to understand people more intensely. In each state or country, the military assigned my husband as part of a Task Force; I would enroll in a Psychology class to comprehend why people do what they do. To my advantage, a broader knowledge gave me the confidence to approach the different races and nationalities, etc., with the Message of the gospel and salvation.

I moved from taking a Psychology class here and there to becoming a full-time Counseling student. My undergraduate credentials are in Human Services Counseling, concentration in Management; a Masters' Certification in Human Services Counseling, a second Masters' Certification in Human Services Counseling/Life Coaching; and am now a Doctoral Student in Pastoral Counseling and Community Care. I am a certified Suicide Prevention Instructor, an affiliate of Yoke Fellow Prison Ministries, and a member of the American Association of Christian Counselors.

As I continued to move about from place to place with the military, opportunities were given to connect with fantastic, unique, and influential people; some were Believers, and some were not believers; Some had not even heard (Acts 19:2). Every connection was beneficial to what God was doing in my life, both spiritually and naturally. I was not conscious of every person and every situation connected to the Will of God concerning me; for that reason, I mishandled relationships, I forfeited opportunities to yoke with those sent by God to enhance me. Upon recognizing my mistakes, the blunders, and the detriment caused by not knowing what was transpiring spiritually, I acknowledge I allowed people to enter into the forbidden areas of my season. I was not protected nor covered from the wolves who sought after my spiritual unborn babes. This horrible place rendered me not knowing who I was spiritually. I was open prey for them that lay in wait for my goods. From the spiritual wilderness position, I sought to know God, to know what to do, how to do, and when to do. I often asked God was there anyone who could help me understand what was not evident to me.

Many of the encounters were too complicated to share. The anomaly of it caused me to be uncertain. Was it something conjured up in my mind, or were these unnatural occurrences happening? I did not know who I could share this position of complexity with and became even more frustrated because of the season of "I don't know, uncertainty, unfamiliar, and what is going on" with me. I found myself letting it go. I felt it was driving me insane to continue with what I could not understand.

Here I am years later, with what I now understand is I needed a Mentor! From a hindsight position, I can say God's plan was moving forward in what seemed like a complete failure. Everything played an intricate role in this area of my life becoming perfected, and we know that all things work together for good to them that love God, to them who are the called according to his purpose (Romans 8:28). Yes, at that time, I needed a mentor. Today, I can say God was preparing me to be a Mentor.

CHAPTER 3

The Experience

Dear Mrs. Angelene Hill

I am writing to say how grateful I am for the mentorship you've given me over the past 20 years. As a newlywed in a marriage doomed to fail, you took me under your wings and encouraged me to see the whole equation. Having the opportunity to learn from someone who has successfully been married for almost 50 years gave me hope that it was possible to make it work. You have shown me that team-work in marriage was the key to making it work. Putting the partner first was a path to improving our quality of life over time. Having you in my life has changed my life forever.

Eternally grateful,
Edward Walker

My Spiritual Mentor

My family and I moved to Germany from the United States in the 90s by way of the military. This place was so unfamiliar to me in so many ways. I could not speak the language, was not familiar with the culture, but most of all, I had no understanding of who

God was. As I became more knowledgeable of my surroundings, I began going to church, and that's where I met Angelene Hill. Instantly we formed a connection in the spirit, and I wanted to know more about the things of God. Through the guidance and the teaching of this Woman of God, she became my mentor. My understanding of the bible increased, and so did my prayer life. We met for noon prayer Monday through Friday. As a young Christian, I never wanted to pray in front of people; I loved to hear others pray, but that's not something I wanted to do. One day it was my turn to pray, and I was so nervous, thinking, what if I said the wrong thing or I can't pray like everybody else. Angelene encouraged me to pray; she reminded me that prayer is between the individual and God. This motivated me so much until I looked forward to those prayer sessions during the week. I remember this one particular prayer meeting I will never forget; I received the baptism of the Holy Spirit that changed my life forever. The meaning of the word mentor is so dear to my heart because when I think of a mentor, and the things I received as a mentee is extraordinary. The person that was in my life as a mentor helped develop my character and empowered my life. The guidance, motivation, and emotional support that this woman invested in me have stayed with me over the years. Now I can invest in others both spiritually and naturally.

Thank you again
Yolanda Wickers

Dear Mrs. Angelene Hill

I am writing to you to thank you for the emotional support you have provided me for the past ten years. As a father who lost his daughter at the age of 26 in a car accident in 2010, I thought my life was over because I blamed myself. Had I been there, maybe I could have somehow prevented it. I asked myself, why did I allow her to get in that car. You allowed me to cry on your shoulders or talk for hours about what she meant to me while you never complained. When there were no more tears to shed, and I ran out of words to talk about, you put me back on track to want to live again. It is because of your genuine love and concern that I am in a better place today.

I sincerely thank you,
Dashaun Ricks

Ms. Angelene Hill

I'm not even sure where to begin. I will begin by saying if you had not answered the Call to Mentorship, I would not be here today to tell this story. As you know, I want others to know that I had decided to end my life; I did not see any hope. Ma'am, you knew something was eating at me, but I would not open up to anyone. I decided I couldn't do it anymore; upon giving up on life, I pulled the razor out to slice my wrist. I heard a voice say, give it one more try. I decided to give it another try and come to church for the last time. I prepared for church, and I decided to put the razor in the pocket of my uniform. When I walked into the sanctuary on this particular Sunday morning, there was a different feel than I'd experienced before. As I sat there with the thoughts of what I would do upon leaving the church, the preacher got up to preach. The sermon was all about me and what I was going through. May I say that I penned this testimony because of Ms. Angelene. Thank you again, ma'am, for being available to save and change my life.

Sincerely,
Thomas Mack

Hi, my name is Karla. I want to say that Ms. Hill helped me in many areas of my life. One major point I want to bring up is that I got pregnant but felt as though I could not have a child out of wedlock and certainly could not raise the child as a single parent. I decide to terminate the pregnancy without letting anyone know. I do not remember how it happened, but Ms. Hill and I were together one day. She began to minister to me about my pregnancy, and I knew it was God speaking to me. She had no idea I was pregnant nor what I had decided to do. I had my baby; he is the most handsome and loveable child you could imagine. Thank you so much for your words of wisdom and for stepping in between me and the decision I was about to make.

Karla

My role as a mentor came into existence by being a spiritual mother to many men and women. I did not consider it as mentorship; I saw the need; I stepped up to meet the need.

A mentor and a mentee is a relationship based on trust. The mentee must feel safe with the mentor, and the mentee must be willing to receive instructions from the mentor.

As a pastor's wife, I stepped into the position of President of the Women's Department in the church my husband pastored. It was by my spiritual nature to assist the women in developing their prayer lives, their roles as mothers, and as military wives.

As I revisit the experiences of that season and reflect on the help needed for development in those areas, it warrants me to understand the need for a mentor. The position of a mentor guides the mentee. As men and women cross paths, the leading of the Holy Spirit and the natural attraction to a mentor create harmony for a successful relationship. As mentioned in a previous chapter, I did not travel a spiritually clear path of understanding in many instances. I was not aware I needed a spiritual map, guidance, "a mentor." On this journey through life, it is essential to know the tools that are necessary and are available for our success. If we do not know which direction we should take or what is needed to go through a season or phase successfully, we can ask our heavenly Father. He will lead us in the direction we should go; it is His Will that we prosper and be in health even as our souls prosper (3 John 1:2).

My military experience consisted of thirty-nine years of moving, settling in, uprooting, and moving again. In this traveling lifestyle, I was afforded opportunities to meet awesome people of various ethnicities, nationalities, and Races. New connections were established, and new cultures were introduced. I grew leaps and bounds in a worldview mentality while experiencing God's glory through creation from multiple angles. Several connections were with people who appeared as ordinary everyday people. It was these whom God assigned to my next level of ministry. Some of my greatest spiritual accomplishments were connected to the people the Lord allowed our paths to cross. From that experience, the wisdom gained is "there is neither Jew nor Greek, there is neither bond nor free, there is neither male nor female: for ye are all one in Christ Jesus." (Galatians 3:28). This scripture became paramount in my perception of people. We do not look the same; we do not act the same; our views are different, our cultures clash; however, we are children of God. It was not an option whether I would embrace someone based on external differences or forbid them the opportunity to become a part of the Mentorship circle God had opened for them. The Holy Spirit was preparing and positioning me for International Mentoring. This opportunity was the gateway that took me to the field of International Evangelism and service as a Missionary. I accompanied a group of Missionaries to Africa to start a ministry in the Gong Hills of Kenya, a place of no electricity, no running water, no toilets, no housing or accommodations American citizens are familiar with. There was no sign of civilization in terms of the lifestyle I and the others were accustomed to. There, in the unfamiliarity, our experience of going to bed was sleeping on the grounds in the field. As we slumbered and slept, the countrymen kept watch over us throughout the night for our protection.

Maybe I should step back a bit to share my story of accepting Christ in my life. I gave my life to the Lord at age twenty-one. I received my primary Christian Education at a Training Institute in Hinesville, GA. Shortly after that, Here comes the next move. My husband received Military Travel Orders for Europe, Germany, to be exact. I said goodbye to the family I made in GA, and I connected to a Body of Believers in Germany. I grew and developed to new heights spiritually and naturally.

I now am sensing the pull of God to Ministry. At this point, I recognize ministry can be done outside of the traditional in the church Pulpit setting.

During the week, I began a noonday fellowship, a Sister to Sister Monthly Meeting, where women united together to sharpen one another. Iron sharpens iron; so a man sharpeneth the countenance of his friend (Proverbs 27:17). From that noonday, a new fellowship was birthed, a monthly Fellowship for Younger Women. This fellowship focused on prayer and why prayer is essential early in life. It drew the attention to the scripture that admonishes us to remember thy Creator in the days of thy youth, while the evil days come not, nor the years draw nigh when thou shalt say, I have no pleasure in them (Ecclesiastes 12:1).

In every geographical location I became connected to, I became involved in a Prayer Group. Today, as I continue in the vein of ministry God has called me to, I still believe in prayer and the changes that come forth from a position of prayer.

The position of prayer is what the believer has been called to; he or she recognizes the pull of God in the vein of prayer. Prayer changes things, circumstances, and it changes people.

The Holy Spirit immediately grasps the believer's heart and carries the believer into the realm of prayer in the moment of a need. The alert given to come into his presence is acknowledged and designed by a vessel yielded through many disciplines. Do not be dismayed if the flesh resists a prayer time; it is known the spirit is willing, but the flesh is weak. Let us continue to embrace II Chronicles 7:14; "If my people, which are called by my name, shall humble themselves, and pray, and seek my face, and turn from their wicked ways; then will I hear from heaven, and will forgive their sin, and will heal their land." We want healing in our land. **LET US PRAY!**

CHAPTER

4

The Mentor In You

"The greatest act of leadership is mentoring; no matter how much you may learn, achieve, accumulate, or accomplish, if it all dies with you, then you are a generational failure."
Myles Munroe

"Leaders don't seek followers; followers are attracted to leaders."
Myles Munroe

"You must decide if you are going to rob the world or bless it with the rich, valuable, potent, untapped resources locked away within you." Myles Munroe

You may ask the question, how do I develop the mentor inside of me? The ability to mentor is a God-given skill and gift. It is innate; it does not have to be conjured up. It does not have to be worked up if it is there. It simply needs to be acknowledged and developed. With prayer and a desire to cultivate the gift inside of you, mentoring will come forth. The scripture tells us, "He that believeth on me, as the scripture hath said, out of his belly shall flow rivers of living water" (John 7:38). When we commit our lives to the Lord, there are gifts, skills, and abilities that come with the anointing. Thus originated the saying, "I am anointed to do this." Simply put, God has given you this, and because of that, you do not have to stress, muster up the ability or have to hope that it comes forth. It is there and evident.

The believer will sense God moving in their lives and seek God concerning what they are feeling. This is the time when you do not allow anyone to tell you what you are gifted to do in the spirit. By this time, hopefully, you know your purpose here on earth. For that reason, you can detect what the Lord has planned for your life. As a mentor, you will find yourself in the position of giving instructions, encouraging people to move forward, assisting people as they attempt to move forward, and giving them directions while they are moving forward. You can receive godly confirmation from another. However, every believer will know or should know what God has anointed them to do. One of the most significant indicators of any gift is that it just flows. It does not take effort. You do not have to ask God to give it to you. He has already placed it inside you! You simply have to go in the presence of God and ask to mature you and your skills. With a heart to please God and a spirit of submission, seek to become more sensitive in the spirit while operating your gift. "Trust the Lord with all thine heart; and lean not to your own understanding, in all thy ways acknowledge him, and he shall direct thy paths. Be not wise in your own eyes: fear the LORD and depart from evil." (Proverbs 5-7).

You may not know that you should become a mentor at first. However, as you become more sensitive to the move of God, you will recognize how the anointing flows in areas of helping people. It is then you will realize the spirit of being a mentor on your life. And, as stated before, consult God for directions. You want to always be guilty of acknowledging God's input. It does not matter how gifted or talented you are. If you fail to recognize and consult God for timing and directions, then you will sail right into a spiritual shipwreck. As a leader, you do not want to be guilty of leading God's people astray or causing them to miss God's hand because of being misled. I always go back to prayer life; it gives me the confidence to move forward with the things that God is saying. It is important to move forward with confidence, knowing God is with us. He hears us. He will give us what to say, what to do, and how to do it. "For this is the confidence that we have in him, that, if we ask anything according to his will, he heareth us." (1 John 5:14). The Lord will speak the things to your heart and spirit that he desires of you. He will give you the confirmation on which direction to move toward.

Working in the field of Community Psychology, you get to see many lives that need help. There are layers of community work to be done. The streets are filled with the homeless and people under the influence of legal and illegal substances. People are hungry for food and hungry for God; or should I say starving for spiritual help and the natural aid is to bandage it with a handout of food or clothes. Now make no mistake, food and clothing are needed, but after giving them food and clothing, what else will we offer them as an aid to the ailment? A spiritual need cannot be satiated with what the world systems provide. Only a spiritual insertion and infusion can accommodate the longing for God the individual is searching for. "Blessed are they which do hunger and thirst after righteousness: for they shall be filled." (Matthew 5:6).

One type of mentor is a Spiritual Mentor. The anointing of a Spiritual Mentor can recognize when the need for something greater is spiritual versus natural. As the areas of need are prevalent, it is often called for the spiritual mentor to move toward the person in need. People will not always come to the help; however, your spiritual antennas are set on the right frequency to detect the unheard cry for help. As you go forth in the earth as vessels for the Kingdom, you are sensitive to the influence of the

Holy Spirit. It is not about how you feel concerning a matter, but how it looks from a realistic perspective. It is about "We walk by faith and not by sight," knowing without a doubt that He leads us in the path we should go. The Heavenly Father wants what is best for humanity; therefore, you can be assured God is in the midst of the earth overthrowing the adversary's workings that is set up to destroy his people. "Let God arise, let his enemies be scattered..." (Psalm 68:1).

As a Spiritual Mentor, the mentee gives the mentor permission to spiritually step into his or her life. However, with the mentee's consent, the Spiritual Mentor can advise in other areas of the mentee's life. The relationship yields trust and honesty on all levels. There is a misconception that a Spiritual Mentor is only needed for spiritual matters. This is far from the truth. They can advise the mentee at any time relating to any issue.

Mentoring can be both paid positions and/or volunteering of services. An agreement to provide services for an exchange of money is consensual between two people. From personal experience, I would categorize the services as formal or informal based on whether there is an exchange of services for monetary gain. On the other hand, community psychologists may choose to provide a service to people of a disadvantaged population in various communities as it is deemed necessary in the helping field or negotiate a cost to provide a service to the community. It is often understood that some services that cater to the disadvantage may not be the going rate, but many providers agree on lower rates because of their willingness to provide the service.

A mentor is revealed either by those who serve various community positions or by an innate desire to share their skills in helping others. In either case, people are desperate for hope; our nation's plight at this time dictates the need for assistance and for those who are community helpers to come forth. A crisis can lead to hopelessness, despair, and a sense of what is the point or what is next. Mental health workers, church clergymen, community care psychologists, care providers, and trained professionals assist in all areas where help is needed. We do not service people based on standards and criteria we set as our idea of who should or should not be serviced.

Mentors are trained to help people, and the helping field is not a place for biases. The mentor has a love of God and is prepared to embrace people from a God perspective. Each area of helping understands the Spiritual Code of Ethics associated with the fieldwork they are assigned to serve. "The love of God is not bound by the walls of religion, denominations, race, nationality; there is neither Jew nor Greek, there is neither bond nor free, there is neither male nor female: for ye are all one in Christ Jesus." (Galatians 3:28). "There is neither Greek nor Jew, circumcision nor uncircumcision, Barbarian, Scythian, bond nor free: but Christ is all and in all." (Colossians 3:11).

As people serving in community service, it is of utmost importance to keep a clean perspective relating to people. Suppose you find yourself judgmental or prejudice toward people and challenged with being fair to everyone regardless of the nationality or side of the track they come from. In that case, it is imperative that you carry this matter to God in prayer. Often prejudices emanate from experiences, upbringing, cultures, and taught behaviors. God created everyone. Heaven is not comprised of sections for differences. Everyone has the same things in common. We all have the DNA of our Heavenly Father. There are no designated places for a race or nationality, elite communities, or denominational sectors. We will all have a place around the throne of God. So, it is on the earth that we do not decide who deserves or does not deserve a service based on differences in beliefs or other diversities. The bible says, "We are the salt of the earth; if the salt has lost its savor, wherewith shall it be salted? It is thenceforth good for nothing but to be cast out, and to be trodden under foot of men." (Matthew 5:13). "We are the light of the world; a city that sit on a hill cannot be hid." (Matthew 5:14). Mentors can be seen afar off because our father is seen through good deeds. A light is produced that is so bright that people cannot help but see it before they get near you. But, it is not us they see. It is the love of God coming forth so strong that his presence cannot be denied.

CHAPTER 5

Who Do You Mentor?

Mentorship is on the rise because of the unlimited amount of the population from different geographical locations in need of services. Technology has provided many methods of communication without limitations to distances. A mentor can meet with a mentee in various cities, states, and countries. The connection and communication via technology offer ease to mentorship communications. The challenges of finding a meeting place and an appropriate time for both mentor and mentee are now obsolete; therefore, the ability to carry out the services are no longer limited.

As mentioned in the previous chapter, whether mentorship is offered in the community or privately, it is a field that needs skilled and caring people. As a mentor, your love for people extends the walls, boundaries, and borders of humanity. There is not a prerequisite nor a preference for who needs help. Those who are called to mentor do not see color, nationality, demographics, geographical areas, males, or females. A mentor sees what God sees and responds as God would have us to respond. "By this shall all men know that ye are my disciples, if ye have love one to another." (John 13:35).

My experiences of multicultural mentoring are always fascinating as I maneuver through the plethora of cultural differences. It is beneficial to the mentee for the mentor to familiarize themselves with various needs. The mentor relies upon the mentee to share, and the mentee must trust the mentor with their story. The mentor is given the information to provide informed instructions or rely on the Holy Spirit to fill in the gaps. I would recommend the inquiry for more information. Have you had the experience someone gave you part of the story omitting intricate parts of the story? Hopefully, the mentee realizes, in order to get the help available they must trust the mentor.

I often share with those I mentor and counsel that I am not in their lives to sharpen any spiritual skills or see how spiritual I am. I also let clients know that I can only give advice based on the client's information. If I make a decision based on what is provided to me, it does not serve as an advantage to them or to me if I am off-kilter for lack of information. May I add, there are people who God will allow in your life; every unfamiliar case can be a stepping-stone to the next level of broadening our worldview. An effective community helper has to be opened to what they can gain to make them more effective and efficient to public service. When we deal with what is familiar, we cannot sympathize with the unfamiliar story. We want to expand our worldview. How will we stretch ourselves to the capacity to make a difference in the earth except we come in contact with the unfamiliar or the new case?

There is an unfortunate reality. There are people who you will not be able to help. When this is realized, you have to release them. You may desire to help them come to a healthy place, but the truth of the matter may be that you were not the one. And that is ok. They may sync better with another mentor. This often happens when male mentors are assigned to female mentees or vise versa. It is even more prevalent in the business and corporate arena of mentoring. Again, the trust factor is the key to connecting and moving forward in mentorship relationships.

How does a mentor gracefully bow out of a mentor/mentee relationship that is not fruitful or productive? How will a mentor know it is not just a hard place in the road that requires patience and perseverance?

How does the mentor advise the mentee to seek help otherwise? What happens when the mentee is not complying with the mentor's guidance and instructions, but the mentor is undoubtedly sure they are assigned to them? These are, but a few questions mentors are faced with in the field of helping. The Holy Spirit is the spiritual mentor to the mentor; He instructs, leads, and guides us into all truths, whatever they are for the one who trusts in him. In the same sense, the mentor relies on the mentee's trust. We trust the Holy Spirit's unction, his guidance, and his instructions. We may not understand all the functions of what is taking place in the relationship, to the betterment of the outcome, we trust our Guide; Trust in the LORD with all thine heart, and lean not unto thine own understanding. In all thy ways acknowledge him, and he shall direct thy paths (Proverbs 3: 5-6). He is the author and the finisher of our faith (Hebrews 12:2).

In the same manner, we trust the instructions of the Guide to inform us what we need to know. We need to know when to hold and to fold. If a mentee mentor relationship is not a match, it serves both parties to know in advance. It is sometimes easily detected that the relationship will not yield the desired outcome; however, it is not always evident initially, but it could manifest itself sooner or later.

The self-matches where individuals choose their mentor is typically based on a pool of mentors that have similar goals and interests. The mentor/mentee relationships could be based on problems or challenges. It is important to properly pair the Mentor and the Mentee. On an informal scale, the mentoring relationship develops from a commonality of interests, experiences, goals, and agreeable personalities. On the formal scale, organizations match a mentor and the protégé for an cultures. The effective mentor cherishes the opportunity of exposure to other cultures. Not only does it open the portals to advancement for the mentee, but it also lends an opportunity for growth and gaining knowledge as you expand your worldview of God's creation and humanity. Mentoring a variety of people supplies the chance to strengthen your skills while amplifying your cultural experience. Knowledge of the subject matters, history, and backgrounds aids the mentor in adequately informing the mentee.

The mentor is not on some type of alert to who they will take in as a mentee. The occasion for mentoring is not known beforehand in many cases; however, there are prearranged agreements made for the mentorship relationship to take place. There are cases when a mentor may gravitate to a pull or an unction to a particular person, organization, or group of people. When this is taking place in the spirit realm, the spirit may be forming a mentor/mentee relationship that only He knows need connecting. I am a firm believer in God moving ahead of time to meet situations on time. Undoubtedly, he went before time to set things in place in time that all things would be on time. "Who truly was foreordained before the foundation of the world but was manifest in these last times for you" (1Peter 1:20).

Some relationships are designed by God; I have heard it put that the relationship was created in heaven, meaning that there is no other way two people could have crossed paths in the fashion they did except God intended it to be. People everywhere are seeking help. They can identify and put their hands on the issues, but they may not know where to look for help or cannot identify what help they need. From personal experience working with clients who have no idea of what they need, I realized that they will ask you to tell them what their problem is. Before the mentor can proceed, it is vital to get the backdrop to the mentee's expected outcome. The relationship may not be a long-term work connection; this relationship may not yield gravitation to the mentee. However, it is often that work relationships require cultural matches. People functions based on their cultural observations, diversity, and knowledge base; they operate in the familiarity of how they have always done things but, in many instances, are open to change.

CHAPTER 6

Finding A Mentor

You are looking for a mentor. What are some of the things you must consider when looking for a mentor? How do you determine if you and the mentor are a good match, and how will you decide whether they are a good mentor?

Let me put it this way, everything good is not good for everybody. What benefits one may cause detriment to another. A prescription may cure the maladies but may bring an ailment to another area of life. With that a good mentor for one may not be a good fit for another. In the areas of interest for mentorship, many things have to be considered when choosing a mentor. Typically, the person desiring to be mentored will not always know what they should expect from a mentor. There are multiple ways to determine if it is a good fit. It could be by word of mouth if credentials are reputable and by online reviews.

A more traditional method of seeking out a mentor is choosing someone you are familiar with and have established a relationship of trust. Recommendation of someone who has a good reputation and seeing results from others who sat under their tutelage or mentoring is a useful way to select a mentor.

In terms of spiritual mentoring, it is almost always the leading of the Holy Spirit to orchestrate a mentoring relationship. We are not capable of knowing what is best for us; however, we know who is. Therefore, we rely solely upon his guidance. One of the things I love about God's instruction is that it is never off or wrong. His instructions are the wings we sail on when the winds of life become boisterous. We remind ourselves and confer with him that he instructed us in the way to take. For that reason, we can ride out any storm with the assurance it will be well. There are mentor relationships that just happen. These are considered informal selections; however, they are deemed effective. Christendom is a powerful platform for mentors to be informally selected. You have church leaders who are influential in the lives of parishioners and people in communities who have significant impacts upon the lives of those whom they serve. Some leadership positions have influenced lives in remarkable ways and are revered as influential mentors throughout the world.

Another informal type of mentorship is when the mentor is not aware they have been selected as a mentor. On a personal note, several mentors do not know who I am and yet scrutinize every move made or word that is said. As a strong mentor, I had to accept that the scrutiny was not an inquiry or a type of surveillance from the individual, but someone watched how a matter is handled. What direction was taken in a case and/or how I carried myself. Instead of becoming emotional, I followed them through social media, listened to godly instructions they provided through the Word of God and their personal experience. These were people who were reputable through character and mannerism, how they handle situations either gracefully or in a distasteful fashion publicly, and the quality of the information they share. Mentors can be used for specific areas of our lives. They can be used for our marriage, business, education, finances, relationships, acting careers, publishing careers, and spirituality, to name a few.

Some mentors serve those in specific Spiritual Callings. For instance, I have a Prophetic Mentor who gauges my ability to hear prophetically, monitors my prophetic utterance precision, and my ability to hear spiritually. I have a Prayer Mentor who checks in with me bi-weekly to see how my intercessory life is developing and what the Lord is saying in confirmation to what He is saying to other intercessors. And I have a mentor who informs me of the many changes taking place in my body, mind, and emotions as I exit one season and enter another season in life. When finding a mentor, consider what you can contribute financially. Typically, the cost varies as it depends on the agreement between mentor and mentee, but the relationship is not formal in many cases. Some mentors do not accept donations of any type and provide service free of charge. Offer a monthly thank you offering to your mentor. It is appropriate to monetarily say thank you, and protocol to sow (give) into the grounds that increases and enhances us.

Regardless of the mentor/mentee relationship being formal or informal, if it does not have a price quote, it is the responsibility of both the mentor and the mentee to have that conversation. Mentorship is a service provided that deserves the honor and reverence that other services obtain. I believe that people would not purposely dishonor or disrespect the gift of mentorship God provided for us. Unfortunately, some of us often do not give reverence to this service as we give to others. Mentoring is a gift from the body of Christ to enhance, instruct, inform, and empower people in the different fields of work. Remember, a hairstylist or nail salon will not provide a service without a monetary exchange. A counselor, life coach, therapist, or any other professional do service in exchange for money. Give due benevolence to a mentor's position, and honor those who spend time directing, instructing us through the perils of life.

On the corporate level, mentors are brought into the workplace to build staff morale and unify the company's goals and objectives. They can assist managers as they work to formulate teams for increased production. Churches also understand the value of mentors. They use mentorship programs to keep departments organized and functioning to their fullest capacities, therefore not hesitating to incorporate a mentorship program into their annual budgets.

So, when choosing a mentor, one must carefully set goals and decide what they desire as an outcome of the mentorship program. From this position, a mentee can hopefully determine who will be a good fit based on what they desire to happen in a healthy mentor relationship. The process of selecting a mentor can be challenging, but fortunately, you can now recognize the signs of being compatible with a mentor you choose.

CHAPTER

7

The Mentor and Mentee

A Mentor and Mentee relationship's position can become more intimate than the counselor/counselee or the midwife/patient relationship. The three relationships carry a level of trust between the two. The mentee develops a higher level of trust with the mentor that suggests he or she relies upon directions in various areas. It is typical for a mentor/mentee relationship to grow from a place of familiarity. Once an agreement is made for a mentor/mentee relationship, whether formal or informal, the two should know enough about each other to consider it safe to form the connection. A formal relationship of mentorship could include the official signing of a contract consisting of the mentor and mentee's agreement. This includes when and where they will do sessions, the number of times agreed upon, and the exchange of money for services. Organizational mentoring, where the individual who is trained to mentor, does so under a contractual agreement framework.

There is a higher level of formality involved. In this case, as with any relationship of information privacy, the mentee may not readily embrace the relationship. It takes longer to build trust. The mentor and the mentee are usually matched up based upon personalities or other compromising factors. With informal mentoring relationships, the mentor provides instructions that will yield results by way of asking questions. The mentee receives instructions by unofficially seeking advice from the mentor. Self-matches are typically based on a pool of mentors that have similar goals and interests. The mentor/mentee relationships could be based on specific problems or challenges. It is essential to properly pair the mentor and the mentee. On an informal scale, the mentoring relationship develops from a commonality of interests, experiences, goals, and agreeable personalities. This relationship can be long term.

On the formal scale, organizations match a mentor and the protégé for an expected outcome. The relationship is not a long-term work connection but is based on their cultural observations, diversity, and knowledge base. The success is determined by the mentor and the mentee continuously working toward the trust factor. Trust is not automatic. The mentor has to be mindful and skillful enough to keep the energy levels of the relationship at an interesting rate. The meeting times have to be acknowledged and honored through the consistency of both parties. It is challenging to maintain a trusting relationship between mentor and mentee when appointment times are not met without communication.

There may come a time the mentor and mentee reach places in the relationship that may become strained. It is the responsibility of the mentee to inform the mentor of his or her feelings concerning the relationship. Both have to take responsibility for the desired positive outcome. If the mentor senses the mentee is not giving enough to get the desired result, the mentor is responsible for making this known to the mentee. If there is no change or if the mentor feels they are not a good fit any longer, the mentor can terminate the relationship with the mentee. The mentor can end the relationship and move on or choose to recommend the mentee to reach out to another mentor. In any case, if the work is not being done and the mentor deems it necessary to remove themselves, then it is to be done with respect and proper protocol. The respectful manner to exit is, to be honest about where the challenges were presented, then make amends. This will allow a mentor and mentee to assess themselves and see where they could have done something different in the relationship.

The beginning stage of the mentor/mentee relationship may feel uptight while both are working towards cohesiveness. Once the relationship is relaxed, the mentee can be eased if revealing to the mentor if an agreed-upon plan was altered. For the mentee, there will be seasons of seeming failure. This is not true. Some adjustments may need to be made while continuing the journey, but there is never a failure. What you see may not resemble what you envisioned, but fasten your heart to the desired outcome. You may refer to these times as delays while moving toward the goal. This will keep your eyes fastened on the objective. For the mentor, the desired outcome is not based on when the mentee's goal is achieved; it is based on ensuring that the goal is actually accomplished. "...The race is not to the swift, nor the battle to the strong, but to them who endures to the end." (Ecclesiastes 9:11). Understand that we are not promised we will advance at a desired rate of speed, but we are promised that we will reap if we faint not. Both mentor and mentee must not grow weary but stay the course. The Promise is at the finish line.

Afterword

WRAP IT ALL UP

In the beginning chapters, I shared my journey through my early years of being a Christian. I was not aware at the time that I needed a mentor. I felt God could not want me; I remember the sinner I once was; how could God possibly want me for preaching. Preaching was my definition of ministry. I was not aware that preaching was not the only thing that God needed people to do for the Kingdom. However, I knew that something was pulling on me that was greater than I. It was the Holy Spirit. It was particularly challenging because I did not know how God called people for ministry; no one approached me to help me understand "it is the ministry that is calling for you."

I finally recognized it was the voice of God calling me into ministry, and I obeyed and honored the Call of God in my life. On numerous occasions, I came to places I did not understand or knew what to do next. It was in these places that I questioned who I was. Was I on the right track? Was it God calling me? How would I do what he wanted and who will help me? I knew undoubtedly I needed help, though I did not know who would help me through this journey.

As time progressed, I understood there were people God raised and continue to raise to intercede through mentorship. The spiritual and natural giftings of God are powerful; they are designed to influence the betterment of those who come under our leadership. With that, mentors not only assist through guidance or recommendations, they are also agents of influence. This characteristic of a mentor is often in search of God's Wisdom to lead others in the ways that are God-Centered and ordained. It is not only the instructions of the leading of the mentor that is prevalent; it is also the mentor's spirit that affects the mentee. The influence the mentor has on the mentee. When the Mentor/Mentee relationship is formed and established, there are intricate things the mentee should know about the mentor. As stated in an earlier chapter, this relationship should be God approved. For a healthy relationship, a mentee should know the advantages of the relationship and study the mentor.

There is a God assigned purpose in the earth for Mentors. Our heavenly Father knows what we need to be successful in every area of our lives. As we consider the need for counseling for someone seeking directions, seeking understanding or revelation knowledge, for that reason, a Spiritual Mentor spends unlimited and countless hours nurturing the spiritual giftings in those he or she mentors. Paul spent innumerable amounts of time mentoring Timothy through encouragement for him to stir up (nurture) the gift of God which was in him; and that God had not given him a spirit of fear; but of power, and love, and a sound mind. As Timothy's spiritual mentor, he saw a need to encourage Timothy. It is recorded in other chapters that Paul admonished him, encouraged him, warned him, and provided him spiritual support throughout his ministry. This is the position of the mentor. When there is a need for impartation, the mentor can assess the need and lead the mentee to the path of fulfilling the need through revelation knowledge. It is especially true in someone called into ministry.

If the mentee presents to the mentor that he or she feels the Call of God into ministry, it is the mentor's responsibility to recognize the gift if he observes the spiritual growth. They must ask God for the insight and instructions to provide the mentee while assisting him in the directions God is calling. Every move and everything that is done has to have the acknowledgment of Father God. The mentor and the mentee both have a responsibility to adhere to the scripture to lean not to your own understanding; we will acknowledge him in all our ways, and he directs our paths.

MARRIAGE MENTORSHIP

People are looking for help to save their marriages or possibly to rekindle the flames of the relationship. Marriages are being challenged from many angles; husbands and wives are under pressure from all life angles. As marriage counseling is sought after, the decision to get help for the relationship as a marriage unit or throw in the towel and let go are the options.

When a couple comes under tutelage for their marriage, they ask for help for many reasons. It could be to become better partners in the relationship, or prevent the relationship from becoming stalled. The mentor may take the course of requesting both partners to look within themselves to find a solution to their problem, or the mentor may ask the couple to focus on what their partner can do to make the marriage work. Both directions can serve as tools for both partners, examining their roles in the relationship's success or failure. During the COVID 19 pandemic, partners can assess where they are in their relationships by spending more time together.

More time together has served partners well; though there are the pressures of life associated with COVID 19, couples in my mentorship expressed they don't spend time together. The wife in the marital relationship shares how the husband does not have to spend so much time at the job site. The husbands share how the wife is not overly stressed with the outside forces as before the pandemic. The workplaces allow both partners to work from home; therefore, couples time together is more than before. The ultimate goal of marriage mentorship is that both partners are able to function as individuals and as a unit. Self-identity is key to confidence in partnership.

For Further Reading

Chapter 1
Exodus 18
    Exodus 18:1-8
    Exodus 18:8
Exodus 3:1
Matthew 12
Esther 2:20

Chapter 2
Matthew 28:19
Matthew 9:37
Acts 19:2
Romans 8:28

Chapter 3
3 John 1:2
Galatians 3:28
Proverbs 27:17
Ecclesiastes 12:1
II Chronicles 7:14

Chapter 4
John 7:38
Proverbs 5-7
1 John 5:14
Matthew 5:6
Psalm 68:1
Galatians 3:28
Colossians 3:11
Matthew 5:13
Matthew 5:14

Chapter 5
John 13:35
Proverbs 3:5-6
Hebrews 12:2

Chapter 7
1 Peter 1:20

www.ingramcontent.com/pod-product-compliance
Lightning Source LLC
Chambersburg PA
CBHW071333190426
43193CB00041B/1766